Where Hibiscus Blooms

And Beyond

Table of Contents

Foreword

Hibiscus is the national flower of South Korea and the state flower of Hawaii.

I was born and raised in South Korea, and my sons were born in Hawaii.

This book is another collection of my memories divided into hibiscus moments and their branching moments remembered in different times and places.

The branching moments are far from the roots. But they chase each other over the oceans from one continent to another breathing every moment. Good enough!

Hibiscus Moments

In the fall, I potted the hibiscus and brought it inside
To continue to bloom--the prominently large red flowers
Opening like time capsules to bring me to the moments
That hibiscus--the South Korean national flower and the
Hawaiian state flower can, for me, raised in South Korea
And having lived in Hawaii for 14 years.

I see each bloom, five petals, and a stamen at the center
Of a slender branch. I hear them singing an old melody
And the silence in between highs and lows, like the peaks
Of valley filling the sky.

I follow the highs and lows of the horizon until I come back
To the tall hibiscus standing at the gate of the invisible
bridge that crosses into the land of poverty among rusty
tanks that we, the children, climbed onto it, and sometimes
We also found the spent bullets—the wreckage of the Korean
War.

So much beauty here and then, remembering the selected
moments, muting and deleting the rest like the hibiscus
blooms fading after a few glorious days, edges of petals
curled—sailing the Hawaiian channels against the stiff trade
wind, and sometimes ghosting along the islands.
Playful purposes accompanied along the sides of our boat.

Life zigzags like sailing between upwind and downwind. My
family tumbled between wars (WW II, Korean War) and
Japanese occupation, and hibiscus bloomed.

The beauty and its shadows like songs with highs and lows--
Births, weddings, reunions, and celebrations on the sunny side
of a coin, while the shady side tells a story begging for
details and revision.

History is strung like prayer beads.

    2023
Year of the Rabbit

Do You Remember?

Buddha In My Palms

I know my way to North River,
Trudging through the snow-covered
Stubbly cornfield to see and hear
Buddha, wondering,
Whose tiny footprints are in my backyard?

January thaw reveals Buddha nature—
Hazy sky spitting snow, mounds of snow on the sidewalk,
And powdery pebbles around the edges of the river.

From here, I see my box-like castle where I eat, sleep, play music,
And write whose space I share with the invited,
And without my knowing, the uninvited sneak in.

Instead, I rush the uninvited to the door,
They come with me to the river
Joyfully romping in the cold pool.
Buddha grins, but I worry about the icy water.

I come home—the potted hibiscus starts to bud.
The woodstove holds red embers waiting for a log.

To my dismay, Buddha grins again at my cupped hands.
They can carry all my baggage,
Buddha nods this time.

2023
Year of the Rabbit

5

Do You Remember…?

Do you remember the walls of the first waiting
Room--the dark and warm uterus
With eyes closed?

Waiting to be born, we were formed
By bits and pieces of wisdom,
Tube-fed and rocked,

Lullabies of small-winged promises
Of crossing the milky way with flutes
Into the vast horizon.

Through the canal, the pale, fragile voice
Announces the arrival into receiving blankets
Held by warm hands in the waiting room
With soft lights.

We don't remember when we are formed,
We are like flower seed pods manifesting
Life in full circle in waiting rooms.

2020
Year of the Rat

A Chipped Mug

Sometimes a chipped mug
Is more than a chipped mug,

Even though it looks like missing
A tooth or two with that faint surface
Crack beneath the gloss.

It still holds tea, warming old hands
With raised blue veins, the flavor wafting
From room to room,

Despite its look, it remembers the original shape
And places where pleasing hands picked it out of the crowd,
Before it sat on a shelf holding pens.

   2020
Year of the Rat

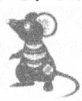

Praise

I praise the sun the way
It wraps my naked skin,
And I praise the earth
For holding me up
Against gravity.

Standing on Earth under the sun
I praise the rainbow,
A spectrum between ultraviolet
And infrared.

Praise the courage to wake up
Defying all the reasons not to.

Call a surgeon to remove
the cancer of fear hiding in dark corners—
Justice mutilated, wrong-doings ignored,
Behind tall forests of daisies
In the slow-growing garden in the summer heat.

Turn on the water for plants
And praise for the growing plants
Emerging out of the soil marking
The silence of the unborn.

I'm perfectly imperfect
Looking for a song between the sun and the ground
Searching for a guiding star on starless nights
To lead me to the path of justice.

I praise the sun rays on my shoulder
That shines both sides of the equation of life.

2020
Year of the Rat

Names

Undisturbed by my last night's
Dream, things stand discretely,
Accompanied by the household
Hummings,

Neither critters nor cold
Dare to invade this fortress
Guarding the names of things
With labels.

Critters with names or without
Are barred from crossing the threshold
Of bolted door, because they don't know
How to knock
On the door.

Notice that even if they follow
The rules of knocking
On the door. They must announce
Their presence by the name in particular twists.

Names frame things,
Fill the dark blank space--
Fear of unpredictability.

We live in a world of things,
We nod and smile at familiar faces
And praise them
By their names.

All unfamiliar doesn't deserve
Our attention. Our arms are neither long
Nor double-jointed enough
To reach the unfamiliar corners
Of the world of things and their names.

2020
Year of the Rat

Shelter

The door is unlatched, always ready
For a passerby seeking a safe place
No need to pry open,
No admission fee required,

Past resentments are accepted
Held by yesterday's hands yielding songs,

Whose lyrics set to a tricky meter
That prevents answers to the questions--
Why fragrant roses have thorns?
Or how to revisit gone-by dirges?

Daylight still seeps through cracks at midnight,
And the sun shelters glistening morning dew
On blades of grass looking for tomorrow.

2020
Year of the Rat

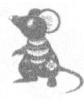

Ramen Noodles

Cheap, crisp, dry noodles out of the package
Into boiling water, then I often add slices of leftover meat,
Egg, chopped cabbage, bean sprouts.

The transformed supple flesh is dished out into bowls
Defying what some say negatively about noodles,
Some depend on these packages that bailout
The economic hardship or busy schedules.

For 14 years, we lived and sailed in the big waters—
Pulling the package out of storage, and making a meal,
Adding wilted cabbage was an immeasurable delight!
Competing for the crown jewel in the land of memories--
Humble life lived simply beyond the map
Of tangled, divisive hemispheric meanings.

2022
Year of the Tiger

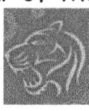

I'm Only

An object for the sun to cast a shadow,
The moon doesn't notice my joy and sorrow,
My height on tiptoe doesn't shorten the distance
Between us.

But I see you pulling tides
And let the tides rip,
You weep when willows lose leaves.

I am more than a shadow,
And my bubbles balloon in joy.
They flatten in sorrow
Hanging on to a sagging string
Waiting for breath to lift me.

I'm more than a shadow
Of an object with a well
Of passion for hope.

Moon, pull me like you pull the tides.

2020
The Year of Rat

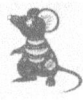

Wildflowers

In October, wildflowers sway in memory;
Waves of pink, yellow, orange, and purple
Dance rhythmically at the will of the wind,
Touching each other, no rules
Of distances between them—
6 feet or 12 feet during the pandemic.

The wind rustles, the river widens
And fall leaves pile up.

I want the vaccine
Against the Coronavirus.
I want the viruses
To stay away from me.
I want to move like wildflowers
In October, November, and deep into winter.

2020
Year of the Rat

I Come from There

I was born over there—
Walking to the muddy confluence to dig clams
From my windowless box house with neighbors on three sides
Along the little winding dirt road that wove the neighborhood
Like vein.

I roamed the river across the street,
Climbing the rusty tank, finding spent bullet cartridges
From the recent Korean War.
Upstream, women pounded laundry on rocks.

I come from there—
We waited in line in front of a spigot to fill our buckets.
We also lined up in front of the public outhouse.

Due to my allergy to dairy products, I stood
And watched the drama of the mobs crowding
The milk truck distributing reconstituted milk,
Hollering, waving their empty vessels.

I played hopscotch etched into the hardened dirt road
That disappeared during the monsoon.

I walked to the elementary school
Where I was introduced to books, papers, and crayons.
There I learned to read and write,
Which became a new obsession.

The new obsession quickly became a lifelong craving
Coloring the blank pages that pleased my family.

Now, I reminisce about the times there,
Sitting here in front of the bow window.
The personal gratification from the deep valley
The sun didn't reach, barely rose to see
The colorful sunrise then.

2023
Year of the Rabbit

Living Alone

Daffodils and hyacinths shrug
Off the dusting of snow in April,

They stand tall in the sun
Between the tingling wires above
And optic fibers beneath,
Perform their obligatory comings
And goings like wind,

They deliver words of life in the countryside.
Many hands dig into the soil
To plant bulbs of hope
And bury roots of lament.

We are wrapped by wires and fibers
Bringing smiling faces and elbow hugs in pixels.
We are separated but not alone,

But I wash my hands alone.

2020
Year of the Rat

Bowl of Inspiration

Love Me

In the valley with peaks and lows
Where rivers tumble, ponds linger,
Time expands and condenses,

Love me tenderly...

Each day is checked off on the calendar,
The day doesn't know it
Like the window doesn't appreciate
The scenery,

Love me sweetly...

Through the innocent windows
The sun rises and sets, painting clouds,

Love me entirely; more than sums of pieces...

When his-story and her-story merge,
The shared stories hold hands,
Then they fly, defying gravity,
Loving the temple of flesh
And bones,

2020
Year of the Rat

The Early Spring Frowns

The unexpected storm buries crocuses
And shiny blades of hyacinths.

You are trapped under the dirty snow.
How can I admire your timely responsibility
To bring earthly happiness?

In that frozen, trapped place
Of the whipped-up storm
Are the invisible bullets of the fear
Of Coronavirus.

The blue mountain swims in a haze,
The early spring frowns
At the mindless jabs in the ribs of the world
Looking for answers.

2020
Year of the Rat

Anticipation

In April, the dreaded snow is gone.
Days are longer; crocuses bloom, daffodils thrive,
And tulips poke through the mulch.
Lilac bushes bud, the dwarf cherry tree
Plans to spread its awning.

April plays the tune for some to march,
Some to waltz, and some to foxtrot.

The river is high, pebbles shine.
Deer are in the field,
Geese honk above in formation.

Every day, patch by patch.
Brown grass is put into motion to paint
The earth green.
It's moving time!

A time of anticipation, planting
New seeds of hope to launch
The old boat in the high river.

2023
Year of the Rabbit

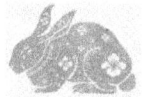

In Quarantine
Coronavirus Outbreak

In self-imposed or mandated quarantine,
Time reels in replay mode,

Cleaning, and organizing again until I am lost
Amidst countless possible efficiencies,
Reading and writing online and between the lines,
Sewing and playing music in an uncertain time.

I practice meditation opening the cage
Of my chitter-chatter and let all go.
A smart aleck rattles the cage and asks,
"Looking for a perfect square without corners?"
Interrupting the flow of flawless time in quarantine,
I elbow it back, "You are no sage!"

Even spring hesitates to open
The wintery door with rusted hinges
In the pandemic.

2020
Year of the Coronavirus Outbreak

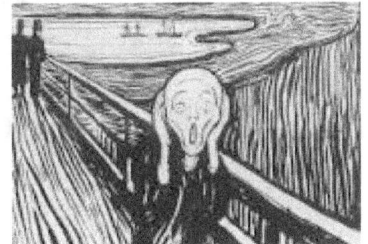

Spring Abundance

Slow, steady rain all day long fills potholes,
Birdbaths and rain barrels.

Between breaks from the rain,
I planted basil, thyme, and red dahlias
Lyn gave me next red tulips from Louise,
And red zinnias from Alice.

Tulips are gone by, lilac bush and columbines
Are soaking up the rain under the grey sky,
Flooding thirsty hearts and rivers
With drops of promises and hopes.

Self-seeding wildflowers thrive along the shore
Of the pebble-lined river competing for specks of dirt.
Even non-natives squeeze themselves in,
And then they become natives in time.

Hopes and promises crowd my river of vein
Dotting in and out of the spring rain, imagining red flowers
In my flower beds. Rain barrels are full and ready
To quench thirst.

2023
Year of the Rabbit

Bowl of Inspiration

In the early spring haze,
Red shoots of peonies
Breakthrough frozen soil,

Tiny primary leaves in the garden
Stand tall, blinking, stunned
After the unexpected snow in May,

Life is a bowl of inspiration.
Big enough to swim in, splashing joy in the sun's warmth,
Dancing with the moon
That lends its ears to our hearts' murmurings.

Let's cast the net far and wide
To catch songs of butterflies
While morning glories climb
Blowing their horns announcing
Their arrival.

This bowl of inspiration--full of gems
In our hands. Fragile but tougher
Than we assume, like little leaves
In the garden.

In the silhouette of the setting sun,
The wheel of day unwinds the thread
 Into the bowl ready for another day.

    2020
Year of the Rat

Measuring Tapes

Out of the toolbox, measuring tapes
Inch their way across kitchen countertops,
Coffee table in the living room
Next to the sewing machine,

Measuring and gauging one, two, three
Dimensions—tall, wide, far
And coil back.

While the fine comb of tape catches fractions,
The fourth and fifth dimensions
Of passions and shortcomings,
Too nearsighted or farsighted
Slip through.

2020
Year of the Rat

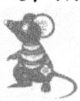

A Blank Page

A blank page waits and wonders
If the wandering words have mounted
The chariot to begin the journey of the day.

The sub-zero arctic blast rages tangoing in woods
Holding hands with one partner briefly and onto the next.

Having its history—from tree to pulp,
A page doesn't censure or grade clouds of our thoughts—
Color, places, after- and forethoughts,
Resentments and moments of grace,
Accepting all the same.

For pages know the importance of clouds
That nurtures trees as much as the sunshine.

2023
Year of the Rabbit

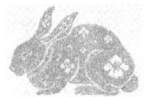

Missing Note

I write following the sound that rings
In my head. Unsure if it's a solo note
Or separated from a chord
Or bass note for humming—
To hum on this gorgeous
Spring day.

Piece by piece, bass and solo notes
Find their places harmonizing
Highs and lows.

Sunshine pours in through windows,
Brings impeccable images of tall evergreens,
Birdbath, and seedlings breaking
Through the soil. A delightful day.

I still look for the sound, a missing note
That has been harping ping and pong.

Things will get easier, Ping said.
And the Pong responds, *Maybe.*

The harp seesaws relentlessly
Filling every nook and corner,
Sparing none.

Writing on this delightful day
Is a joy despite the missing note.

2023
Year of the Rabbit

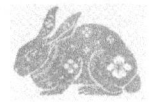

Gift of Time

Happy New Year-Ritual

We rise out of bed to begin the day like machines
After the night's rest to meet the demands on hand—
Biological, cultural, and ever-present emotional needs.

We are the cultural machine that weaves fiber into a fabric—
Ether into infrared like heat exchange—
An era of incredible technological innovation.

I resist jumping into the new era,
Like changing soft, warm pajamas with slippers
For day clothes with shape-fitting shoes.
But time has no sentiment for the setting
And rising of the sun.

My resistance keeps my pajamas on all day long,
This invasive demand for change is relentless!
My poor eyesight even fails to follow the delicate movement
Of the needle.

Raking through my seven decades of sunrises and sunsets—
A mere minuscule drop on the planetary timeline,
I wonder what the tines of the rake brought home,
Leaving the rest behind.

Happy new year, from Year of the Tiger to Rabbit!
Bring me a pair of magnifying glasses—telescopic, bifocal,
Or otherwise, and a duffle bag full of what the rake
Left behind.

2022
Year of the Tiger

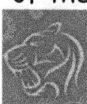

Raking

At the end of a fretfully hot summer,
I'm awed at brilliant foliage—red, yellow, golden,
Big and small leaves among the tall, somber evergreens.

Days are shorter and cooler.
It's time to rake the leaves,
Leaving limbs bare.

I raked for days, loading them onto a tarp,
Dragged to a place for compost
Losing their shapes and colors--
Like dust in the wind.

Between dusk and nightfall,
The little solar lights on our window sill
Remind me of the cycle of life—
Far, near, short-term, and light years.

I participate in the cycle. I deny it.
I direct the composting piles,
And close my eyes for the dust to pass.
Each moment I close my eyes brings me closer
And being raked, recycled.

I still rake as winter practices its first snowstorm.
Impossibly beautiful day—
Each dark oak leaf blown in mutters stories to each other.
But I don't hear them. I'm standing and raking
Letting my denials pass through the gaps of tines.

2022
Year of the Tiger

Word Salad

Beets meet fern fronds and fiddleheads from ponds
In a large wooden bowl in the company of diverse greens,
Goat cheese, walnuts, and cherry tomatoes.

No dressing needed, for they are just words,
Words for justice and aching hearts.

Cherry=picked words please taste buds
And refresh the fading song,
"Where has love gone?"

I chew tender fibers of greens
While the music shifts its tempo--
Nibbling yesterday today.

2020
Year of the Rat

Time

Is time an avant-garde percussionist
That beats at the edge
Of the forward direction only?

Or does the time burn moments
Whose ash renews the soil for the seeds
Of humankind?

Time keeps track of my minuscule role
On new and old orbits that chip away
Shaping the boulders of the thundering universe
Bringing a tsunami of joy and grief.

In the deep pool of my life,
Grains of rice that have shaped me
Can't separate from the loaf of bread
That's my existence now.

Time in patterned hemispheric spaces
Holds life as is--the fragrance of lavender
Wavers across the drawing line of searing lightning.

How does time echo back across the ages—
A smorgasbord of flavors and tastes?

2020
Year of the Rat

In Mid-Summer

The spring flirtation is gone by,
Cosmoses dance in the bright sun
After a downpour, alliums fade,
Daylilies count days before school starts.

Today with the help of nostalgic comfort
Of blinding hopes, finds a way to move forward,
Despite the weight of shadowy scars
Of yesterday marked with welt.

Does mid-summer dream the late summer,
Fall, and beyond? Intoxicated bees buzz
Over bee balms, love-struck,

It's mid-summer.

2020
Year of the Rat

Retired

Retirement barreled down the steep hill of Covid,
Too old to pole-vault the pandemic wall, but not too tired
To scatter the ashes of the last night's fire in the woodstove
To look for buried embers to restart fires.

The kindling catches sparks,
The flame dances flamboyantly,
Leaving its meager start behind.

Retired with no mandated schedule, I refuse to be dust
in the wind, but dream of embers beyond the lid
Of the sarcophagus to bring the flame of heroes
And heroines to weave them into the floating fiber
Of my daily living.

Retired, feeling the pinch and dizzy
When provoked and spun around.
My time-tested marbles still roll and move--
Old and still human enough.

Retired, I define the way I plow the field.
No longer looking for a square for my round pebbles.

2022
Year of the Tiger

Walking On Stilts

I was taught to worship the art of walking on stilts
By memorizing social rules derived from Confucius's times
Leaving no space for my needs.

We break our toes to fit
Into the unforgiving, rigid wooden shoes
Of shame of traditional and cultural imperatives
By shaving toes. I believed in the rules. Regularly, I washed
my hands
With the unsavory soapy dysfunctional
Indoctrinations.

We share the scars of the ownership,
I still hear the fading drum beats
Out of tune, out of time, and out of place,

Let's bend the will to walk on stilts,
We want to jump and run
Chasing after dreams and ideals
Gurgling in our inner wells.

2020
Year of the Rat

Singing In Dark Times

We need to sing in dark times
Soprano, alto, tenor, baritone, even falsetto
Professional or amateur.

Sing in the difficult times, piercing
Through the tunnel with no end in sight,
Where we are all amateurs not knowing
Where our feet will land.

We are professionals in life
Just because we are born,
And sing and dance in dark times
Even in the pitch-dark bile
Seeping out like oil drips.

Every step forward brings us closer
To the light at the end of our dark tunnel.

    2020
Year of the Rat

The Navigator

My Son-Stevaki (1970-1990)

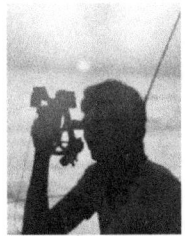

He peers through the sextant
Bringing the wobbling sun
To the horizon, minute calculations
Culminate in a line of position—
Somewhere on the chart,

Where the Mother of Pearl lost her pearls
Still looking for yesterday, green with envy
Of others keeping their pearls.

Find me--a shriveled rind on a nameless shore--
Like unsettled dust of fading memories
Of her pearls,

Navigator, finding me
And tell me our positions.

2020
Year of the Rat

Evening

Sets in as daylight fades,
Geese honk in the grey sky
And then, life walks into poetry.

I pick Swiss Chard in late October
Sweet peas still hang unto flowers,
No time for peas to ripen,
But it's never wholly lost
For life progresses,

The evening is too dark for some,
But for others, it's the beginning of a day.
Evening sets, towing daylight behind.

2020
Year of the Rat

Gift of Tide

Questions Arise

In luminous hours—
Are you decent to others?
Do you love others whom you may never see?

Sitting on the fence in the glaring sun
It's easy to turn my head
And choose what I want to see
Squelching the pleas of need,
Replacing them with my justifications;
what I do and what I don't do,

Not admitting how my being here participates
In a wasteful way of life
At the expense of others
I may never see—

Many excuses in my storage bag--
Some plausibly convincing,
Some full of errors in plain sight.
I discard them as soon as I can.

Do I love fellow humans--far and near
And practice compassion even in small ways?

    2020
Year of the Rat

A Dogged Tide Of Thoughts

I cross my legs—not my mind, sitting
Next to the bay window holding a notepad.
I see a family of turkeys looking for breakfast
In the morning haze across the street.

A dogged tide of thoughts rushes to my shore--
Why, what, and when...?

No answers, only small thoughts,
But come as you are in your old soft-soled shoes
Of memories and desires.

Life is contradictory. My little raft
Riding the long river crosses
Many lands with many tongues
Adding, subtracting, and rewriting histories.

The tide retreats to big waters
Leaving a line on the sand,
Meanwhile, I uncross my mind,
When the answer will come.

2020
Year of the Rat

Gift Of Tide

My children came knocking on my door like the tide
Bearing the gift of unrehearsed motherhood
In their soft skin.

Motherhood without instructions--
But a bayonet on one side
And a sword on the other,

Motherhood cleared away the debris on my path
Left behind by the war long ago.
It held an umbrella over the children
In rain and harsh sunlight.

The sky was cerulean,
Crystal-clear water in the trade winds,
No need to be war-ready,

The Cold War was else-where in unmarked lands,
Its distance guaranteed the safety
Of shining pearls with soft skins
And babbling voices.

Motherhood makes music in continual crescendo,
Until it diminishes like a retreating tide.

2020
Year of the Rat

49

Dancing Ghost

On a slowly simmering summer evening,
Mist descends to rest in the river below,
What ails you, Dancing Ghost?

The fragrance of lavender wafts,
Lilies are ready to burst,
Morning glories are waiting to blow horns,

And the cosmos is pondering
To open petals to see
The strings of chaos wrapping
Around stems.

what ails you and me
Beneath the muted passion?

Our disabled and yet primarily abled
Worn bodies, young at heart,
Manifest times and seasons gone by,

Some memories are in the shreds of fibers
And some in the flowers in the ether--
The remainder of joy and sorrow.

What ails me is that I failed to marvel
The flowers that bloomed
From the seeds I planted,

And I failed to harvest seeds to plant them
The following spring in the very same soil.

What ails me differs from yours,
But we carry the same pail of time
Carrying different waters of joy and sorrow.

What does it take for us to carry pails without spilling?

2020
Year of the Rat

Laughing Again

History repeats itself--
The sun rises in the east,
The moon pulls tides,
A bruised heals.

In bittersweet life,
When the flesh is bitten off,
The peach pit looks for soil,
The moon and sun keep their orbits.

But be mindful that time never repeats,
The river returns in a different form
Guarding its essence.

We laugh again when the peach sprouts
From a pit, remembering the sweet flesh
Between our teeth.

2021
Year of the Ox

Knitting

We sit in circles, knit, and purl, balls of yarn roll,
Focused eyes catch kinks, run them between fingers
To be curled again—new locks to warm hands, heads,
And hearts.

Daily knitting and purling following patterns,
Checking and counting stitches iron out yesterday's knots.

Knitting and purling--casting stitches, binding off--
To a piece of fabric—some stiff and some pliant
Depending on the fiber--warm and water-repellent wool,
Water-absorbing cotton and others in between,
The array of yarn is abundant; almost as many hands
Knit and purl, darning broken dreams one stitch at a time.

2022
Year of the Tiger

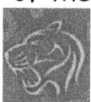

Covid

When the perimeter of my life
Caves in saving 6' feet around me,

I will be a nightingale or hummingbird
I will dance and howl under my guiding star.

In that orbit of dreams
I will build a grand runway
To a broader world,

To survive and go on beyond walls,
And rules of self-preservation.
I'll look for perennials that outlive
Annuals.

2020
Year of the Rat

Dust

At 74, nearly three-quarters of a century old,
I'm sitting in front of our wood stove.
The flame dances, ignoring 19 degrees outside,
Erasing winter in New England.

My thoughts are bobbing around, riding the inner current
From the doldrums, the counter-current against the
prevailing trade wind.
Our sailboat rocked, and its shapeless sails flip-flopped.
The halyards banged against the mast. Anything not tied
Down or wedged in, rattled in the cabin. Big waves from
Faraway places rocked us relentlessly. A shark circled us,
cutting through sparkling, hushed blue water under
Blazing sun. Our boys shouted, "Shark!"

The trade wind lost its grip,
Occasional crashing waves scattered dust sputtering
Sputtering the beginning, ending, and middle of a brief song.

In the dark, cold morning, far away from the doldrums,
I was so willing to go to places so far away, so long ago...
Maybe to repaint the images--
Maybe to ease the speed of light--
Before the corrosion invades the lock
Against our will, remembering the counter-current
In the doldrums.

Dust we live in,
Dust we breathe in,
Dust we eat,
And dust we become.

    2023
Year of the Rabbit

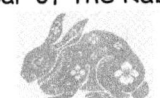

Funnybones

Am I Listening?

The potted hibiscus bloomed during the February arctic
blast. Was I listening to their joy preparing for the opening
ceremony?

My inner chatterbox works overtime without compensation—
Busy daily chores, and still on duty during the night
Directing my dream. I toss and turn and sleepwalk.

Seeing the colorful morning sky, I hear,
Red sky in the morning, sailor's warning.

Do I listen to the warnings, signs of war, and peace
Quieting down the incessant chatterbox of talking heads?

I shuffle between the pleas of the distant unknown
Drum beat and the knock on my door.
What do I hear? Do I listen to the joy of being?

2023
Year of the Rabbit

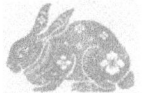

I Feel Grateful

For the twenty-six letters--
How unfathomably deep and far they reach
With the alpha-numeric combination.

Everyday writing does not exhaust them.
They line up even though I have
To cheer them up by chiding
"What's up?"

I'm thankful for not having to learn
Another language where I might have to move
My arms so much that the shoulder joints
Wear out and wriggle my thin eyebrows.
I may never be able to communicate
To my heart's content,
For thin eyebrows tend to have pale voices.

Just imagine a big boat carrying
Twenty-six letters and numbers 0-9
Sailing in the vast star-studded universe,
Spelling names of billions of people,

Even my foreign name found a small place
In the lineup of the alphabet.

2020
Year of the Rat

Finding Kindness

Finding kindness, moments of grace
Inside and out, look around
Near and far, through
Darkness and sunshine
In sleep and awake
Not one second passes by
Gush...a gyroscope might direct us disguised in

Kilt or Kimono, kidnapping
Inside out, outside in
No one knows which
Direction it's heading
Near and far, maybe
Eternity has seen the struggle—déjà vu.
Sigh...
Smile, and hug...

2023
Year of the Rabbit

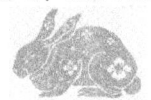

Funnybones

How did funnybones get their name?

There is nothing funny about them,
A knock causes pain and makes the mind
Mindless, numb, and tingling
Trying to soothe the ulnar nerve entrapment,
Holding the arm checking fingers.

Funnybone, a hard-to-spell scientific word
Causes pain even to pronounce it,
And they are not bones at all from the spine
Traveling to neck, elbow, and fingers.

Life jostling funny bones perform their duties
In spite of the misnomer--
Are not funny at all.

2020
Year of the Rat

Dusty Road

Every morning, a cup of decaf coffee smooths my throat,
But unsure what else it touches,
As I walk the familiar dusty road--
The world at large looming on the horizon.

My being, microscopic at best, without deadlines
To meet—but there is a deadline for all living beings.
I hoped to be excluded from such a broad definition
By being especially small, a microscopic being.

A pipe dream—I saw my mom dying wasted
In her cancer-driven body, her wish unfulfilled.
Grandma passed away when I was away from Korea.

Time doesn't wait for any microscopic excuses
Continues to roam every nook and corner of a dusty road.

2021
Year of the Ox

Going Somewhere

When I was young, a long time ago,
I believed that the only direction of the life force
Was to move ahead, paying scant attention
To where I was and who I was then.

Move ahead written in big letters—
Bold, capitalized, even though there was no capitalization
In Korean. It was part of the grand scheme of the game--
Moving ahead by adapting to anything new
While recoloring my quiet, old foundation.

I jumped onto the bandwagon, joining the chorus
Lip-synching, doing my part, clutching navigational
Equipment—Sextant and parallelogram getting the position
Translated into numbers--
Some big with many zeros,
Some minute fractions.

Now in my advanced age,
I no longer peer into the sextant
To watch the glowing sun get to noon latitude,
Noon has long passed over my head,
But its image remains.

No numbers direct me now,
And my feeble feet carefully tread
The slippery, icy winter roads
Hoping that spring finds its way.

    2022
Year of the Tiger

Lost In Pandemic

Lost in political bickering again,
Shouting from the opposite
Sides of one road,

When and how to reopen businesses
After the mandated closures
For public health—
The threat of Coronavirus.

I'm confused; no one stands
In the middle of the road,
The narrow margins packed
With biases leaving standing room only,
Sucking oxygen from the center.

Lost like a boat adrift after the storm--
Helpless in soundless dreams
In a sealed vacuum.

I'm confused and lost,
How I can do anything correctly, unaffected
By the bullets of biases and collective beliefs,

Can I get through the hours now
Without crumbling the wall of time?

Is there any time to lose?

    2020
Year of the Rat

A Late Bloomer

On chilly November days, the last rose hangs in
Without blankets but thorns,
Most perennials have gone to bed till spring,

Rose's thorny defiance jabs at the clock,
Shaking pointer fingers at the mercury, demanding
Not to slide. It wants to have one more fling--
Swinging hips and fluttering little leaves in the breeze
What's left on her branches.

She refuses to talk about her story—too many prickles.
She wants to see the clock sweeping
Its arms one more day.

My empathy for the late bloomer rises—
The abrupt ending of season-long cuddling and caring
Of little leaves and buds.

   2021
Year of the Ox

Flammable Planet

I watch the Ukraine war unfold on a flat screen.
My helpless feeling brings me back to the war-filled story
Of my family and me, a two-year-old during the Korean War.

Who would remember the quick dance,
The shuffle of losses and casualties,
And the ember under ash?

Despite the changing venues of broadcasting news,
The goal of war stays the same--terrorize, burn,
And destroy bricks and flesh.

I cry when I see women carry children through rubble,
When I see old women walk with small bundles in their hands,
When I see the smudged faces of hungry children.

I cry, you cry, we cry on this flammable planet!

What do I remember from this "Blitz-Krieg" that destroyed
A nation and its people? How does history remember
The aggressor and victim in a war?

So much on fire between children's tears and political
propaganda, which leaves truth unexamined.
War doesn't remember.

2022
Year of the Tiger

Good Enough

Morning

The morning haze peels off,
Trees stand tall in the blue sky,
The breeze rustles the leaves.
A herd of turkeys is out for breakfast.

Morning, a beginning
To walk into broad day
To cast a shadow of dream
What might it be?
A coup d'etat of mind?

Sun rises shortening the shadow of the wood,
What else is yet to be unveiled?

How many mornings are in a day?
How many beginnings are in the beginning?

2020
Year of the Rat

River In The Sky

The pouty sky unplugs and lets
The river in the sky drain
Into the brook across the street
To launder the grey blanket,

Pounding and scrubbing it on a boulder
And then hang it in the sun and wind,
In the field full of trees
Where the brook weaves
Through tall grass and wildflowers.

If I had a pair of wings,
That harp, ping, and plop,
I would fly to the River in the Sky—
Pineapple Express from Hawaii to California,
To watch the stirrings below the surface,
That have been burrowing since the invention
Of words and history.

If I can't find my wings,
I can't move the field, the trees.
Then we can have foliated memories
Of the field in my journey
With boulders carpeted with moss
Where amphibious love sings
From here to up above.

2020
Year of the Rat

71

Being There

From here to there
And from there to here--
A simple arithmetic addition
Or subtraction in meters or feet,
Where plains are plains
And mountains are mountains.

My fancy spreads its wings
And soars from here to there
Or return from there to here--
The Plains of Peace,
Caves in Mountains.

Ask the globe-trotting air
Engulfing the moving planet,
Who neither adds nor subtracts,
To differentiate here from there.

Be mindful of being there and here,
Then there would be no additions
Nor subtractions
Eliminating the differences.

2020
Year of the Rat

Good Enough

Where is "perfection"
Where shame shies away,
And only reappears redressed?

I read burning pages of social fabrics
Fraught with eloquence, elegance, and eminence
That my blood lacks,

The ashes of a flaming soul
Pulsating in my narrow artery
Are good enough to engage with the conscience.

Good enough is as perfect
As life on this evolving earth,

With open hands and arms,
Stand still till birds start resting
On my open palms,

And that is good enough
To open my and your hearts.

2020
Year of the Rat

Empty Rooms

Words leave our lips
Finding new waves in renewed light,
Having brewed for a long time,

To find a new home with empty rooms,
To start another beginning
Free from scars of old memories.

A beginning, a chip off an old block,
Fills empty rooms to mend broken hearts,
Sweetening bitterness, rubbing ointments
Into sunburnt knuckles.

Sailing around not-so-empty rooms,
The chip off the old block leans on a table,
Waits for the departed words to come back.

2020
Year of the Rat

Weeding

I pull out weeds from perennial flower beds
On a hot June day where protests
Against police brutality spread
On the streets of this land.

Irises and Solomon's Seal prosper in my flower beds,
Deemed to be desirable, I'm careful around them,
And add a layer of mulch.

But even some desirables get weeded out
Since they can't control their impulsive invasiveness.

Protests persist on the streets,
The powerfully uniformed hold shields
Against unarmed people in all colored skins.

My brown skin is scared and hides in flower beds.

2020
Year of the Rat

Sailing On Top Of Mountains

Have you heard about sailing
around the globe on top of mountains?

In the sea of uncertainty,
The wind leaves the canvas drooping,
Stalling the boat on the distant horizon
Where low tide exposes rocks,
And green algae dry out in the sun.

The wind whistles through evergreens,
And deciduous trees wake up the river,
Unfurling the stories of storms at sea
While the wind clings to the sides of a mountain.

The moving sea finally comes to rest,
Taking deep gulps of breath in thin air,
Still sailing furling and unfurling
The folds of tattered sails.

2020
Year of the Rat

76

Fall Foliage

From spring to fall
Deciduous trees and evergreens
Climb sides of hills and mountains
In heat and wind,

Planning the season of flickering flame--
Red maples and sumacs,
Yellow ginkgos, orange honey locusts,
Around evergreens with stern wicks,
To engulf the swaggering summits,
To tease wondering eyes.

In the waning harvest sickle moon
I know what's up with the rustles
Of falling leaves preparing to be composted
For the revolving return of primary roots
And seedling leaves.

Flamboyant leaves dance one more time
In the red sky, following the stream of wind
To woods, unable to resist the pull of gravity.

Like falling leaves, I too shall march
Through the invisible gate of woods
To return to the home
Where one finishes
And the other begins.

2019
Year of the Pig

Gold Panning

A schemer stands in a creek panning for gold
Shifting a pan, looking for shiny nuggets,
Gold-coated illusions under shallow, deflecting water.

Wild schemes of get-rich darting in and out of the cloud
As big as Pangea—the age-old supercontinent
Before the breakup into tectonic plates.

Then the plates drifted apart.
Stealing some gold,
Leaving chaos behind,
The remaining gold hidden in rivers
And dark crevices.

Through the revolving doors of evolution
Emerges schemers claiming independence
Dismissing the age-old interdependence
Of the planet and humanity,

The wise shakes the index finger scornfully
Between the lines of history.

2020
Year of the Rat

Heart To Heart

Unborn silence like untold stories
Live in the wombs of hearts.

Yesterday begets today
May flowers remember
April shower but forget
Dark clouds.

Long beads of silence tell
Births and what's still in labor,

What's to be held in cupped hands
And cherished from one heart to another.

2020
Year of the Rat

Acknowledgment

Many thanks to Mary Clare Powell for editing and teaching me how to ask questions and unpack invisible details.

Thank you, Louise, Emily, Faith, Janet, Nancy, and Carol for your support.

I owe many thanks to Henry who helps me navigate the world of computers.

Self-published books by Yenna Yi

Ring of Fire (Memoir)

Poetry Books

Star Dust

Unvarnished Life